Copyright © 2017-2018 Matt Powers
Original Title: *5 Steps to an Abundant Future.*
1st edition ISBN-10: 0-9977043-4-9
1st edition ISBN-13: 978-0-9977043-4-1

All Rights Reserved.
Written by Matt Powers.
Cover & All Photography by Matt Powers
unless cited otherwise.
Formatted by Matt Powers.
Send all Inquiries to:
Matt@ThePermacultureStudent.com
or
Matt Powers
PowersPermaculture123
28419 SE 67th St
Issaquah, WA 98027

Published and Distributed by PowersPermaculture123.
Printed through IngramSpark Publishing.

Please Note: The information in this book represents research from sources listed in The Permaculture Student 2—it is an educational and informational resource and does not represent any agreement, guarantee, or promise by any party associated with the creation or editing of this book. This book and its information and sources are not designed to diagnose or treat any medical condition. Consult a licensed physician for medical treatment and advice. The publisher, editors, and author are not responsible for any negative or unintended consequences from applying or misapplying any of the information in this book.

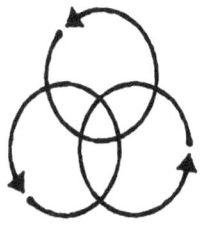

Table of Contents

Introduction: A Holistic Collapse (1)

Step 1: Build Soils (4)

Step 2: Grow Forests (14)

Step 3: Restore the Oceans and All Water (20)

Step 4: Regenerate Biodiversity (26)

Step 5: Rewild Human Culture (32)

Conclusion: The Future (43)

About the Author (50)

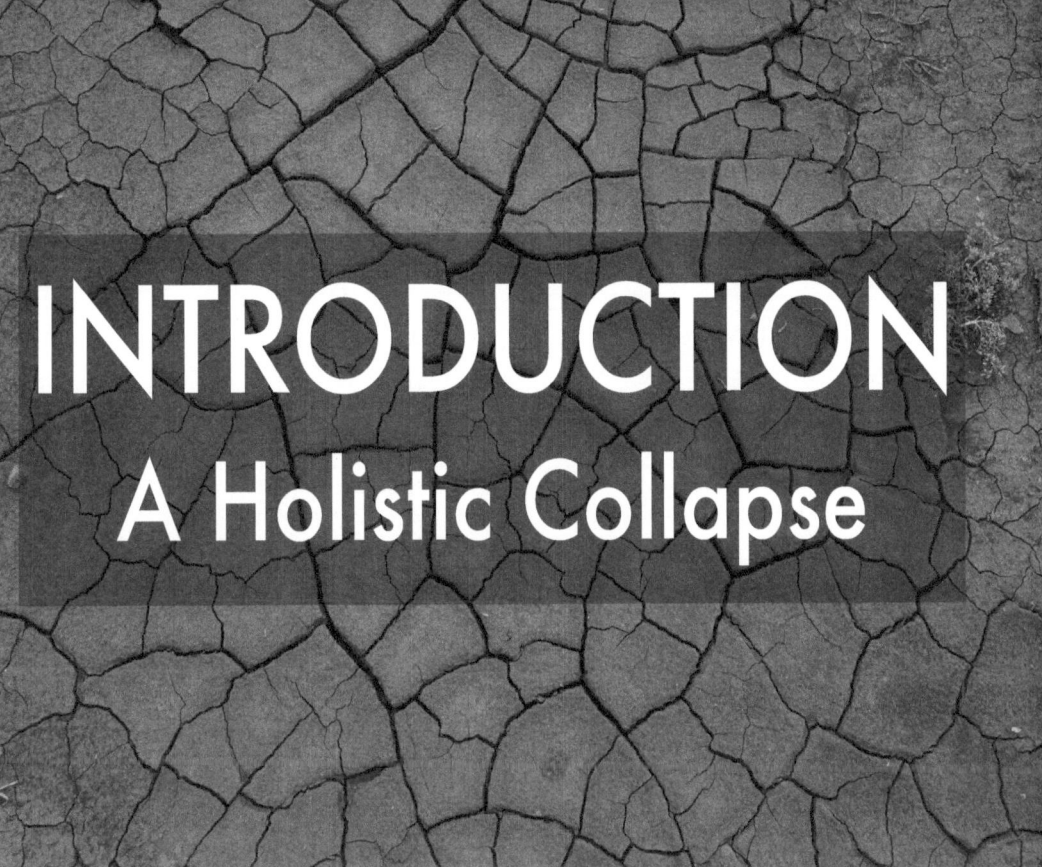

INTRODUCTION
A Holistic Collapse

The Economy! The Environment! Politics! Health! Society!

Turn on the news, and it's immediately in your face - the fear, the panic, and the utter lack of hope. The belief that we are doomed, damned, or destined for extinction has become pandemic. It has infected religion, culture, entertainment, science, governments, hearts, and minds across the globe, and in a way, it is a self-fulfilling prophecy. *If we believe we will fail then we will fail* - that much is certain, but what isn't certain is if we can reverse the imbalance - if only because it is uncertain whether we will all change and accept a new story together.

What you aren't hearing in this dystopian fear-based hallucination is the truth, the reality, which is that we can regenerate and restore our environment; we can stop the destruction that we call the status quo both in the environment and our cultures. We can stop funding the wholesale destruction of our collective future and start funding and co-creating a future of regeneration and abundance. That's what natural systems provide.

In the holistic context we call *nature*, all biodiversity, economies, governments, sciences, social systems, and all that is human and not human take place. If we partner with the same systems that created and maintained the world into which humans came to be in, we will find stability and abundance. We can reboot the natural world before it erases this current operating system and adopts a new framework in which humans and most mammals cannot thrive.

Climate change is very real & exponentially increasing in tandem with many of its indicators such as desertification, deforestation, habitat loss, mass extinction, global average temperature changes, ice melt/sea rise, etc. All climate change is related to imbalance in the environment and a

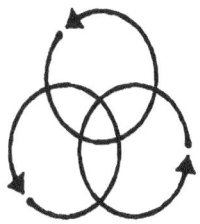

Table of Contents

Introduction: A Holistic Collapse (1)

Step 1: Build Soils (4)

Step 2: Grow Forests (14)

Step 3: Restore the Oceans and All Water (20)

Step 4: Regenerate Biodiversity (26)

Step 5: Rewild Human Culture (32)

Conclusion: The Future (43)

About the Author (50)

displacement or degradation of the foundational systems of a biome: soils, forests, waterways/bodies of water, and biodiversity. Human systems have degraded or destroyed these foundational pillars to our environment globally - we've logged or burned all forests to a small fraction of what they were, we're driving one of the largest extinction events in planetary history, we've destroyed the majority of the world's topsoils, and we've poisoned and imbalanced the air and the ocean's systems. In geological history we've seen natural examples of destruction at the scale that humans have wrought in modern times, but it's rare, isolated, and a temporary reset of natural succession while what we are doing is more akin to a comet hitting the planet.

What is in this short book is a plan - a series of steps that need to be taken if we are to reverse the damage and pull back from the edge of extinction. They are steps that imply a great amount of change in the way we behave and think as a species globally, but if we do these steps and evolve past scarcity thinking and embrace syntropic thinking, we will find the future waiting for us is abundant and exponentially bright.

STEP ONE
BUILD SOILS

Return the Carbon

Have we released an irreversible amount of CO_2 into the atmosphere? That is the constant question these days. Have we crossed the tipping point that will plunge our natural support systems into chaos? We do not know, but many fear we have already — yet, atmospheric carbon dioxide levels still retreat each year from choking the skies in later winter and early spring to being absorbed entirely by plants by mid-summer.

Field corn alone can sequester 400x the current annual carbon increase in the atmosphere each year (97% of a corn stalk is made of carbon from the air). We can never sequester everything back into soil - even with biochar, but we can greatly reduce its loss by using different methods. Conventional farmers will till or spray their fields with salt-based, petrochemical fertilizers and biocides, desiccating the organic matter and soil life. The lack of fungi and soil life in general prevents the carbon

The Loess Plateau in China

(which is soil organic matter) from staying in the soil. Tons of carbon can be sequestered per acre - that means feet of soil can also be generated per year. New understanding of soil life and site design as well as new technology like nano-clay are allowing for the greening of deserts. All of our desertified regions can be turned into productive perennial agricultural areas, & instead of releasing carbon, they will begin to sequester it in leaps and bounds. This can be done in only a few years time as was done with the Loess Plateau Restoration Project in China which started out as only 15,000km^2 and ballooned into 500,000km^2 and changed

The Loess Plateau in China

Chinese law altogether leading to an incredible regeneration of rural China. We can reverse our course with atmospheric carbon incredibly quick if we make a concerted effort to build soils (raising organic matter levels) - there is plenty of room in the depleted soil bank for atmospheric carbon to be sequestered. We can take back all our emissions and more.

Yet how is this possible? We've seen studies saying you CAN'T do this - they've tried it in fields in Iowa and California... or so you've heard or even read. The problem is dead soil, or more accurately 'dirt', doesn't perform the normal natural functions of living soils. This doesn't even account for the high level and amazing natural functions of soil that are possible in certain contexts with high levels of biodiversity and organic matter present. One way soils can accomplish this is through Arbuscular mycorrhizal fungi (AM fungi); it is responsible for a third of all carbon sequestered in

our soils globally in the form of soil structure (the carbon glues that hold the soil together and give it its loamy texture) - in the Northern temperate zones it can account for 47% of the carbon in the soil. Yet 'conventional' agriculture relies upon anti-fungal biocides, heavy tillage, and synthetic fertilizers all of which release carbon in their manufacture and usage, destroying soil organic matter and structure. Hence, those fields in Iowa and California that are just dirt cannot hold the carbon. AM Fungi is also just one player in the fantastic economy of the soil that fungi and bacteria facilitate.

Half the excess CO_2 from the atmosphere has been absorbed by the oceans. This has caused a slight increase in pH (making it more acidic though it's still alkaline). The acidification of the ocean is preventing crustaceans from forming complete or strong exoskeletons and shells; it's bleaching the coral reefs as well. In a setting where cancer was once considered an impossibility in nature, we see it present and spreading in marine animals more each year. The oceans have their own soils as well as a fungal foundation that facilitates the oceans decomposition cycles. It is in the animals, plants, soils, and microbiology that we must sequester the carbon in the oceans - we must have an enormous increase in ocean biodiversity. There is no better place for this excess carbon, and it is our only feasible and proven solution for reducing atmospheric and oceanic carbon levels.

NoTill, LowTill, & NoKill Farming

Would you believe me if I said 'tillage', or more accurately inversion plowing, is the leading release of carbon into the atmosphere? You can see how carbon dioxide concentrations change over the course of an entire year on a publicly accessible NASA video online. If you watch it and watch the months and locations, it's very clear where emissions are coming from, but if you don't know what to look for it may seem confusing. Though the video explains why **all the carbon dioxide gets sequestered each summer into plant life and soil**, it fails to explain why each spring the most carbon is emitted. It is the time of tillage, spraying, and heavy machinery for farmers across the Northern  Hemisphere. They are undoing what the plant and soil life did that summer before. They are tilling the soil, breaking that structure down and aerating it so it oxidizes and releases carbon into the air. They are spraying their fields to kill back those 'weeds' before they plant - those biocides kill soil life and release carbon. Synthetic nitrogen fertilizers are salt-based and they destroy the soil structure and organic matter as well. When they harvest, they compact the soil further and even if they are conventional no till and leave the plant residues in place, they will mostly oxidize and release that carbon back into the air - they will spray the plant residues with biocides as well, increasing erosion, compaction, and morbidity in the soil. As can be seen clearly by the video of our planet, our cars and even our fireplaces are not making a dent in comparison to what conventional agriculture is doing.

As soils lose structure they become compacted or erode - they wash or blow away. We have lost nearly all of our topsoil worldwide. Many 'experts' hold that only a 5-6 decades remain of topsoil. The very thing we are destroying is the only way we can maintain ourselves.

As an alternative to traditional methods, we can seed directly into native grasses and get a competitive crop yield - it's called Pasture Cropping and Col Seis has been doing it for over 20 years. You can follow the harvest, which can be done with machines, with cattle to mow it down fully for reseeding.

We can grow organic no-till where we either are planting directly into mulch, in small, open pockets, or using a seed drill to avoid soil disturbance. We can use strategic low tillage options like Keyline subsoil or chisel plowing to break up hardpan and heal a landscape's hydrological functions, or, if really needful, harrowing to gently turn-till the top 3 inches or less of soil for planting annuals (since they rely upon disturbance) - but better than harrowing for annuals is to develop a perennial food system. The point of this litany of methods is that it's not only possible but folks are doing it out there right now and succeeding in making money and feeding people with these methods.

Revegetate to Reverse Desertification & Reserve Slopes for Vegetation

To fight erosion, we can imitate China's example with an outright ban on grazing slopes 20% or steeper in all of rural China with a focus on edible revegetation methods using hand-made earthworks. It has ended hunger and economic depression as it has ended erosion, carbon-release, and habitat loss. The common solution to all those issues was 'perennializing' the landscape and their food system.

This was also the case for Kenya where deforestation and conventional agriculture were continued even after the colonists were free from the colonizers - they'd forgotten how to rely upon their natural perennial systems. Wangari Maathai's work earned her the Noble Peace Prize, and it all centered around planting trees. She led a female cultural liberation movement, challenged the oppressive and corrupt government, and eventually served in Kenyan Parliament - even instilling a love and reverence for trees in the military of Kenya - in her efforts to reforest the landscape.

We will also see similar tandem successes and gains as we bring back biodiversity through revegetation and reforestation. We must green the cities, the areas of desertification, the exposed soils of conventional farmers, and our coasts.

Evolve from a Annual-based Diet to a Perennial-based Diet

Cultures based around perennial staple foods are more enduring by design - in a bad year an annual farmer may lose the entire crop and not have enough seed for the following year, but a bad year for an orchard is less traumatic. Trees are more resilient than annual crops. In arid or desertified climates, trees can go years without rains while even perennial grasses cannot endure (which means that grazers and browsers come 2nd to trees). If we do not cut or disturb the ground at  all, we more thoroughly sequester carbon into the soil bank. Perennial agriculture is carbon farming by design.

STEP 1 BUILDING SOILS CHECKLIST

%	Task
☐	Plant Trees
☐	Composting Kitchen Scraps
☐	Buying Perennials
☐	Growing Perennials
☐	Buying NoTill Organic (or LowTill/NoKill)
☐	Growing NoTill Organic (or LowTill/NoKill)
☐	Composting Cardboard & Paper Waste
☐	Growing Mushrooms on Waste
☐	Sheet Mulching
☐	Cover Cropping/Green Manure
☐	Crop Rotation
☐	Using Compost Tea or Extract
☐	
☐	

*Learn more in **The Permaculture Student 2** available on ThePermacultureStudent.com

STEP TWO
GROW FORESTS

Regrow the Forests

Our planet once had vast primeval forests, enduring old growth, and thick vegetation where we now have deserts, cities, and agriculture. Bringing back the forests, longterm storages of carbon, will help balance the atmosphere and stabilize weather patterns and seasonal cycles. Forests and trees generate rain, steadily store carbon as they build soil, provide habitat, reduce erosion, and mitigate the surrounding climate - forests also help filter, hold, and slowly release water. The biodiversity upon which we rely and are

adapted and evolved to survive with came to be in a world with vast, rich and diverse forests across its surface. For our longterm survival, we must bring back the forests.

    The oxygen used to be higher in concentration in our environment (since there were more plants and animals embodying more carbon, and more plants releasing more oxygen). Cities today are areas of low oxygen concentration - likely in part why bottled air is remains on sale in China's areas of extreme air pollution. By bringing back trees and

vegetation in general we can raise oxygen levels while we lower carbon dioxide levels.

    The ideal clean, perfectly mineralized water for our consumption primarily comes from landscapes that are holding water at such a heavy capacity that they release it in purified springs. Rain water is like naturally distilled water and leaches minerals from us while well water is usually high in minerals and can cause a mineral imbalance overtime and cause health problems as well - springs provide the ideal balance most often.

Trees also create shade which cools soils and prevents carbon from being released. Their shade extends the lifespan of snow cover and allows snowmelt to occur at a slower rate - preventing flooding and erosion as well as extending the winter season and its effects - organic matter decomposes under winter snowpack and feeds the soil. Uncovered organic matter will oxidize, releasing the carbon into the air.

Large-Scale Community Restoration Projects

While it may sound inconceivable, we can restore our forests despite our track record of destroying them - humans in general have changed their behaviors and beliefs collectively and individually consistently for as long as there have been humans. We are adaptive beings. Reforestation also might not be new - there's evidence that we extended and helped generate large sections of the Amazon rainforest using earthworks and canals though we cannot but speculate how extensive their work was.

Fortunately we don't have to guess how the Loess Plateau was restored in China. The Loess Plateau is the birthplace of Chinese agriculture and after thousands of years of cultivation and then grazing, they desertified and eroded it. It was restored by the people of the Loess Plateau themselves using simple permaculture and holistic management techniques in under ten years: handmade earthworks, perennials, withholding grazers on brittle landscape slopes, and giving control to the local people over the landscape.

In the Kingdom of Saudi Arabia, the Al Baydha project has proven that restoration can occur with much lower annual precipitation where droughts go on for years with no rain. The entire Arabian peninsula's coast can be turned into productive perennial food forests, and eventually they could be grazed using careful holistic management.

In areas with state and national schools systems, all school children could be educated through their direct involvement in reforestation projects - from tree nurseries to earthwork creation to seed saving to silviculture and beyond. Government employees of all stripes all over the world could be enlisted in the

In only a few years' time, vegetation has claimed the swales completely, leaving no bare ground in the swale beds at the Al Baydha Project in Saudi Arabia.

effort to reforest our world - anyone can participate in this work. We must inspire all organizations to evolve, regenerate, and restore - no matter their prior function or associations.

STEP 2 GROW FORESTS CHECKLIST

%	Task
☐	Planting Trees
☐	Using Keyline/Swales/Berms/Earthworks
☐	Growing Perennials from Seed
☐	Rooting Cuttings
☐	Silviculture (Managing Forests)
☐	Starting a Food Forest
☐	
☐	

*Learn more in **The Permaculture Student 2** available on ThePermacultureStudent.com

STEP THREE
RESTORE THE OCEANS AND ALL WATER

Ban Ocean Harvesting

Did you ever hear that we've nearly fished yellowfin tuna into extinction? Or did you ever read that we're emptying the seas, raking the sea floor clean of organisms? The oceans *are* becoming deserted, polluted, and dysfunctional. Have you also heard of the acidification of the oceans caused by diffusion of excess atmospheric carbon into the ocean waters? To avert complete collapse of ocean biodiversity as we know it, we must resist the urge to harvest anything from the ocean while two things occur: the ocean populations

surge back and the manmade contamination and diffused carbon from the atmosphere get cycled into the ocean soils, bound together in an inert form. Once ocean populations are dense, then cycling of toxins will occur quickly - toxins will quickly be diffused into the biology rather than focused into cancers and die-offs.

    If we do not want to be the filters for the contamination and face negative side effects like cancer or dysfunctional immune systems, we must allow nature to cycle and store those toxins. If we want healthy oceans in the future, we must preserve the dwindling biodiversity and abstain from supporting any ocean harvesting now.

Keep it Pure

There is no reason to allow any exceptions for dumping anything that can harm or contaminate a body of water ever - water is life. Pure, clean water must be protected - dirty or contaminated water needs to be cleaned, restored, and then protected. All water leaving any site must be clean and safe.

Protect & Generate Life: Artificial Barrier Reefs, Vertical Farming, & Wetland Restoration

To restore our oceans we need to support them in regenerating themselves. The coasts are where most of the ocean life resides or is born. It is a critical biome. If we are to support and regenerate the oceans, shores, and coastal wetlands, we need to support, protect, and spread natural habitat.

Artificial barrier reefs shelter coastal regions much like a windbreak does on land - these can be seeded with life and minerals like a Biri Bud. They provide habitat within themselves and create an edge effect which increases the species present by at least threefold. If vertical or 3D ocean farming is used inside and outside the artificial barriers, it will magnify the nutrient and mineral cycling and biodiversity through edge and shelter effect.

In addition to the shores and coastal waters, we must rewild and restore the wetlands, streams, and rivers leading to and from all bodies of water. Wetlands filter and clean waters, sequester incredible amounts of carbon, and provide habitat for innumerable organisms. Inducing meandering in our artificially straightened rivers,

A Biri Bud is the seed of a future reef.

recreating flood plains in areas where it has been removed, and recreating lost wetlands all need to occur.

If we can bring back the life along these coasts and get them to ecosystemic capacity, we will see the system itself as a whole expand to accommodate more life by building upon its foundation, the soils of the ocean. As on land, we must sequester carbon, build soils, and restore biodiversity - the path towards regeneration is the same.

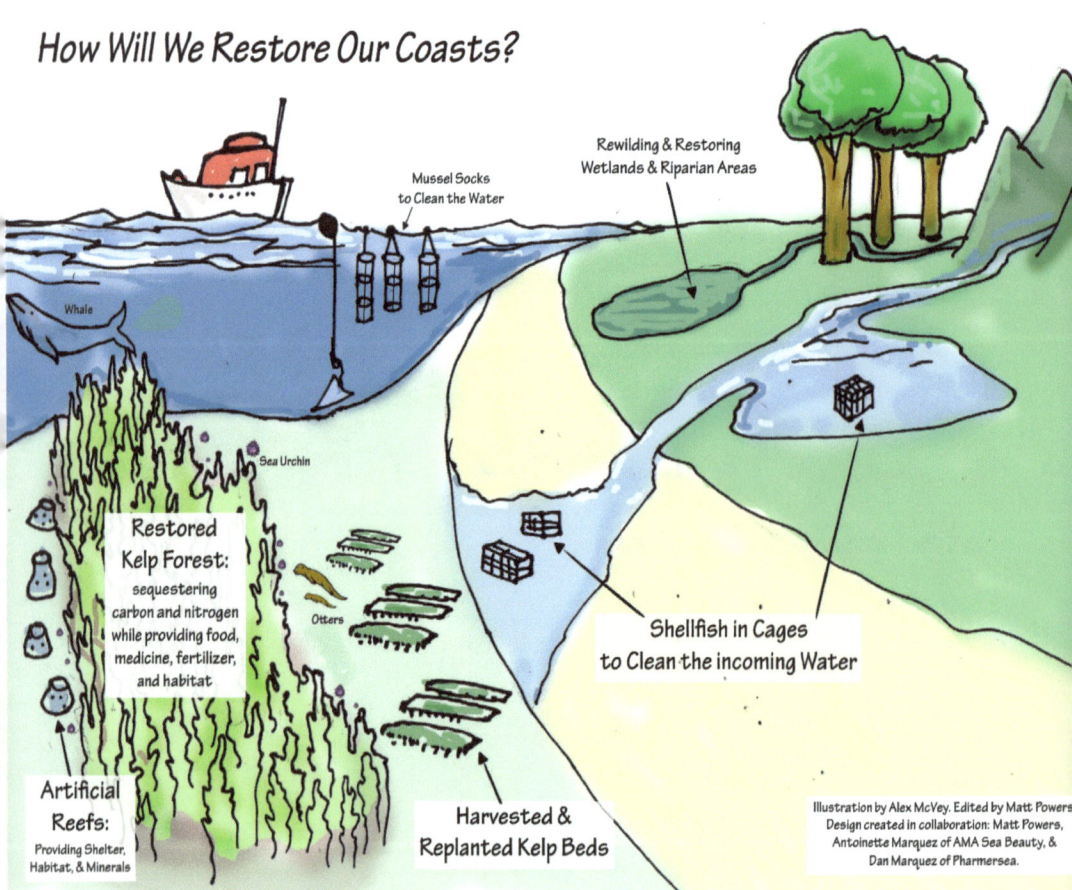

STEP 3 RESTORE THE OCEANS & ALL WATER CHECKLIST

%	Task
☐	Treating Graywater on site
☐	Treating Blackwater on site
☐	Using Rainwater to Offset Water Usage
☐	Rewilding Wetlands
☐	Rewilding Riparian Areas
☐	Rewilding Streams/Creeks/Rivers
☐	Building Habitat for Ocean, Wetland, Stream, & Riparian Biodiversity
☐	Cleaning Up Pollution & Trash
☐	Slowing, Spreading, Sinking, & Saving Water that Enters the Site
☐	Avoiding Ocean Harvesting
☐	
☐	

*Learn more in **The Permaculture Student 2** available on ThePermacultureStudent.com

STEP FOUR
REGENERATE BIODIVERSITY

ReWilding

    To rewild is to bring something back into alignment with nature. For many it may sound a disturbing concept since we've long demonized nature itself and literally waged war on it, but we must instead reverse full thrust and start setting up self-managing ecosystems, building resiliency in ourselves as well as our plants and animals, and removing manmade impediments to nature which are currently nearly ubiquitous. If our economy's purpose was solely to rewild with every purchase or transaction, we'd likely still need to involve all levels of education and government in the effort to remake our tamed and dying world into one that is wild and vibrant. Regenerating our lost and waning biodiversity starts with rewilding our landscapes, our systems, and ourselves.

Seed Saving, Plant Breeding, & Perennializing of Annuals

We have lost most of the genetic diversity of our vegetable and fruit crops in the past 120 years. We must preserve, grow, and seed save what heirloom seeds remain

Impossible Purple Speckled Peruvian corn is comprised of corn deemed impossible to grow in North America by the leading experts, but by crossing two "impossible" varieties in a microclimate that mimicked their southern hemisphere's daylight patterns, I was able to make the impossible possible.

Huauzontle growing in 140F/60C temperature soils without irrigation in the middle of California drought.

even as we breed new varieties in hopes of replacing what was lost (which took generations upon generations to generate). Luckily, today we have more people than ever to help in the effort, living in a diversity of climates with access to a greater diversity of seed than any global generation in human history has ever had access to.

In addition to saving and breeding, we need to adapt as many of our annuals as possible into perennials. Perennials do not require soil disturbance and continually generate biomass which leads to perpetual soil creation. Annuals require some disturbance though it can be minimized through simple technology like the Peruvian chisel, called a Tacllas, or by planting by hand like Ruth Stout's method for planting in sheet mulch.

Most importantly, perennials offer the 'wilder' selection of the two. They are more resilient and prolific, and they create a greater and longer- lasting benefit over time. Currently there are efforts to rewild greens, such as tree kale, grains of various sorts, and fruit trees with true to seed heirloom varieties. The overall picture of biodiversity loss over the past 10,000 years is directly related to agriculture and humanity's spread (though the end of the ice age 10-12,000 years ago had its own natural repercussions on biodiversity) - if we are to reverse the current extinction rates, we must switch to perennials as the core of our diet to reverse the soil loss and rewild our diets to support local native biodiversity even as we must restore and rewild the wilderness.

Raising, ReWilding, & Breeding Animals

Animals both domesticated and wild are dwindling in diversity, and wild animals of all types are shrinking in number as well. Where once megafauna and megaflora proudly grew, we now have desertification spreading like a global cancer. What heritage breeds that remain we need to raise and breed in the most wild and natural manner possible to strengthen and spread their genetics. We also need to reintroduce displaced wild species to their former bioregions and recreate their original habitat - removing manmade obstructions may be vital to this process. Some areas where animals have long been extinct that are needed (like the missing Mastodon), analogs from other biomes may be introduced and even adapted to get the needed ecological effects.

STEP 3 REGENERATE BIODIVERSITY

%	Task
	Growing & Saving Heirlooms Seeds
	Breeding New Heirlooms & Landraces
	Saving & Spreading Native Seeds
	Providing Habitat for Biodiversity
	ReWilding Natural Habitat of Biodiversity
	Raising Heritage Breeds of Animals
	Breeding New Varieties of Animal using Heritage Stock
	Including Native Plants & Animals in our Diets
	Removing Manmade Impediments to Natural Function from Wild spaces

*Learn more in **The Permaculture Student 2** available on ThePermacultureStudent.com

STEP FIVE
REWILD HUMAN CULTURE

ReWilding = Freedom

For many, the idea of wildness immediately generates a negative response - wildness equates to chaos in popular conception, even though it is from this wilderness that all humanity came and this same wildness that has been supporting humanity's entire existence.

What is wildness or wilderness at all? Wildernesses are self-managed natural landscapes where biodiversity has its own cycles and systems that sustain and spread life.

Perhaps the closest analog we have in human systems to rewilding is personal freedom - the ability to freely choose for yourself how to live your life. That is what we are proposing for nature and large ecosystems including the ones we live in. It could also be seen as direct democracy as in the way that small communications between all the birds in a flock determine their movement - though from the outside, it appears to be uniform like that of one organism or mind. Unplanned cities also self-generate in this manner.

Tempering our human concepts of freedom is the recognition that the laws of nature are our actual boundaries regardless of human laws or freedoms. True freedom needs to be seen in the larger context as self-managing to regenerate and generate benefit to both people and the environment exponentially over time. There can be no human conception of freedom without a healthy environment and rich biodiversity to support it - there neither can be any form of civilization without abundant natural capital which is currently rapidly dwindling.

The boundaries we set on wilderness and wildness have always generated desertification and extinction - it's time to reverse thousands of years of domestication of both ourselves and the ecosystems we effect. It's time to embrace wildness and generate wilderness.

ReLocalize our Economies to our Biomes

All fiber, food, fuel, energy, & medicine need to be generated regeneratively within the local biome. That means that population sizes need to be within their biomes capacity (or within their own capacity to provide for themselves within that biome). When we are no longer on a fossil-fueled economy, we will find quickly that the solar and soil economies have limits - we naturally will align to those availabilities as we have in the past when civilizations collapsed over night - we flee to a place that is more fertile. The only problem is there are no longer any places to flee to.

Instead this time, we must not flee; we must dig in and reverse the damage we have done using the sun, soil, fungi, animals, and plants in our bioregion only. That doesn't mean we cannot use what resources we have now to quickly usher in this new regrarian age like using alternative energy bridge technologies, but we must move quickly and sequester more carbon than we release as we do it and from then on move beyond fossil fuel derived bridge technologies.

Part of relocalizing our economies will be embracing entrepreneurship to fill the role that large, global businesses are currently occupying. Innovation and job creation will explode in tandem as solutions are made biome-specific.

Decentralization of Governance & Currency

As with nature, so with mankind - we must self govern and be free to be regenerative as we see fit. Both our systems of centralized governance and economies from borders to paper bills need to be firstly examined for their efficacy and then primarily relocalized to the regional biome. It should be noted that trade always was and always will be in nature and in human systems. Currency - paper bills or bits of gold or silver - is an anthropological concept as well and exists outside the laws and systems of nature. It is a symbol rather than a reality. Governance is similar - it reinforces a social construct that is a socially recognized fiction rather than a reality. They are both social games being played, and their rules can be changed or abandoned.

The concept of the 8 forms of Capital recognizes other forms of capital in addition to financial capital (currency) - these are social, fiscal, living (nature), cultural, experiential, intellectual, spiritual, and material. Decentralization will allow for diversification and adaptation to local needs and limitations - these other forms of currency will become increasingly important as communities relocalize.

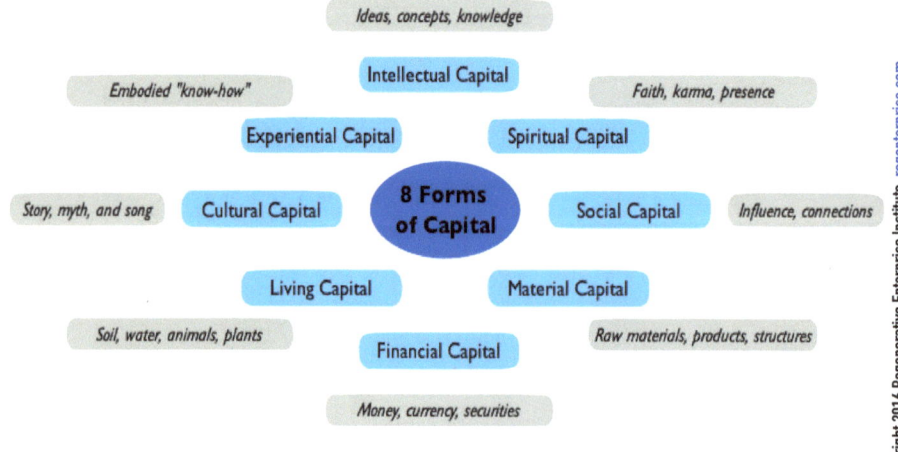

Unschooling Education

Education is the main cultural transmission mechanism - though entertainment and media are a near second, they are more changeable and responsive to cultural shifts. We are still stuck in an imperial British educational model where individuals are trained to be an interchangeable cog in a large centralized empire where uniformity increases productivity and makes management easier. By simplifying education and our world itself, to be understandable, we have generated and supported a weak counterfeit of both. We've created a monocultural human culture.

Education should be an exploration of the world by the learner where teachers are facilitators and guides on their journey. Grading, testing, busy work like homework, age grouping, compulsory education, only focusing on lower level cognitive skills, only focusing on verbal (reading, writing) and logical (math) skills, violent communication patterns (in contrast to NonViolent Communication), dictatorial hierarchy that extends from lawmakers to administrators to teachers to students, and withholding children and youth from active outdoor play, learning, and exploration - all these destructive and damaging practices must end for education to be a liberating process for children.

No one can force someone to learn - whatever is being forced upon the student will be shunned, hated, and quickly forgotten as much as possible. The experience of learning is more important than the learning of any set of information or skill because without a positive learning atmosphere and experience where students are truly free to leave, disagree, pursue a new direction, or delve deeper, nothing will be incorporated with enthusiasm which is the highest level of engagement and represents the greatest potential for creative application and thorough understanding. To liberate ourselves, we must liberate our education systems from imperial, dictatorial, centralized, and bureaucratic patterns.

In addition to how we school we must change what we are teaching. Our educational backbone must be permacultural, that is, focused on regeneration through natural patterns and systems using the lens of the three ethics: care of earth, care of people, and care of the future. Schools should be outside, in nature, and focused on natural order, regeneration, and pattern literacy. Through that lens, all history, science, technology, and analytical skills find appropriate place and limitations.

ReDesigning Homes, Infrastructure & Transportation

Our homes, our cities, our towns, our streets, our transportation, and everything in between has to stop being environmentally degenerative and instead be regenerative for it to remain in place. We cannot make this larger global systemic change unless we make these smaller changes in our daily lives, our communities, and in the greater structures and systems of humanity starting now.

Our homes must generate power instead of require it. They must store heat when we need it and shed it when we don't. A properly designed home will collect and purify water, let in light to minimize the need for artificial lighting, and grow food as a natural function of waste processing. A home should enhance the environment around it even as it provides for and shelters its human inhabitants. Luckily, there are both historical and modern examples that fulfill these requirements. All we need to do now is retrofit our cities to enhance the environment as a whole (even when construction and raw material energy inputs are considered).

Transportation too must change - as we relocalize our consumption and production, we will dramatically reduce the need for large-scale transportation. Bicycle powered cars are more and more common with some that even go as fast as fossil fuel powered cars. Gliders and solar powered planes are also increasing in their efficiency and sustainability. A regenerative option for transportation might include animals as well - horses, oxen, goats, dogs, and more. Materials for all these devices can easily be harvested from our surplus of landfills and garbage dumps.

Limitations to Consumption & the End of Waste

Above all, we need to limit our consumption of goods and services to strictly regenerative sources. We need to eat food from farmers who are building soil. We need to source building materials from recycled sources or sustainably harvested materials (like bamboo). We also cannot endlessly consume; we must produce to offset our consumption as we limit our choices to ethical ones.

Part of limiting our consumption to ethical sources is the end of waste as we know it. There can be no more garbage - there never was an 'away' in 'throw away'; there always was a place the garbage was being thrown. Usually plants and

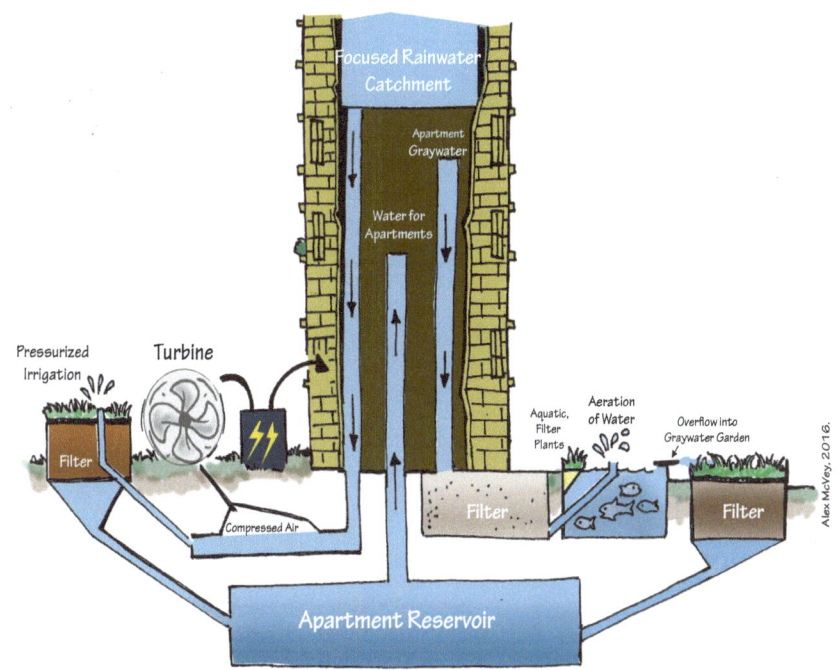

Rainwater catchment from larger buildings could be routed and focused into smaller building systems for energy generation, water pressure, or graywater usage.

animals are occupying those spaces before we established them for dumping, but sometimes people are displaced as well. All our waste must become a resource in another beneficial cycle.

STEP 3 REWILD HUMAN CULTURE

%	Task
☐	Using Alternative Energy Solutions
☐	Growing a Garden
☐	Growing Mushrooms or Fungi in General
☐	Raising Fish
☐	Raising Aquatic Plants
☐	Fermenting Foods
☐	Time Outside
☐	Time Supporting the other 4 Steps
☐	Supporting the Local Economy
☐	Running a Local Business
☐	Using Alternative Transportation
☐	Raising Animals for Food, Fiber, Dairy, etc.
☐	Growing Fiber Crops
☐	Spinning Fibers into Yarn and Thread
☐	Making Homegrown Clothes
☐	
☐	
☐	
☐	
☐	

*Learn more in **The Permaculture Student 2** available on ThePermacultureStudent.com

CONCLUSION
THE FUTURE

To the Doubters

You may say: you cannot change the financial district and their grip on financial legislation, or you cannot change the banks and their grip on mortgages and banking legislation - or you can use that same pattern of doubt for any aspect of any positive proposal by almost anyone anywhere, but the facts remain: many, if not most, civilizations and societal patterns and laws that were once considered unchangeable fell into obscurity due to lack of natural capital in their environments - we are about to face a rapid global decline in natural capital that is all precipitated by our own actions, and we have to prepare to combat or mitigate their effects.

The Mayans assuredly thought their economic and spiritual systems immune to extinction yet buildings were abandoned half made when their civilization collapsed - people forgot the social constructs, laws, religions, and fled into the jungle. There is no jungle this time, and there are too many of us. We have to pre-empt our mindless flight to nowhere and instead dig in, be responsible for our own actions, and regenerate where we stand.

Living Permaculture

We must live our ethics: care of the earth, care of people, and care of the future. Permaculture seeks to create this alignment - it is both something new and something old as it recognizes a pattern of human alignment to nature as a common thread throughout time that thickens as we travel

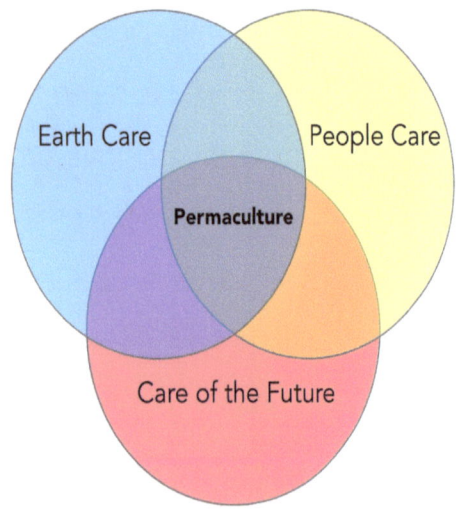

backward and becomes the fundamental way of life in pre-agriculture and pre-fire usage times. If we can use permaculture as a lens for solving our problems and living our lives, we can recreate our culture into a regenerative, beneficial force.

Permaculture Politics

There are seemingly three paths to political change: violence, legislation through petitioning governance, and abandonment. The most effective by far is abandonment - the forgetting is often complete. Often with violence it doesn't lead to new patterns, and often with legislation, the laws can just be changed again or reinterpreted. Lasting change is found in abandonment - as in a rewilding movement where self-managers turn their backs on the past and start working on the future with complete focus. The best foot forward will be to spread the 5 Steps themselves and to start NOW on making them a part of our lives and communities. Laws, traditions, and human systems that interfere with regenerative change must be abandoned as we race to regenerate our world before it is too late. Others may continue in these negative patterns but they will feel out of place - the more we abandon and embrace the empowerment of regenerative living, the more will be called to follow the trend.

Forging Change Fast Enough

Is there enough time? Among those keenly aware of our predicament is a growing sense of dread and despair, but that has more to do with the action of analysis than it does with the analysis itself. They are not actively working on making the change a reality. We have jobs, bills, laws, and a rapidly changing climate - it feels overwhelming and outside our control, but it isn't. In fact, we are the only ones that can make the changes needed in time.

To do this, we have to include everyone. That means we need to talk, share, and include our neighbors, strangers, enemies, families, coworkers, and friends. Start a local 5 Steps group to educate and spread the ideas - include all the regenerative workers from your area: permaculture, agroforestry, holistic management, natural farming, biointensive, etc. Form alliances, new local economies using alternative forms of capital, community gardens, seed swaps, local fiber, local medicine, and more. Start to transition away from the centralized patterns - relocalize your food, get off the electrical/gas/water grid, buy locally, raise your own animals, grow soil, and more. The idea is to start and spread the concepts. Once the ideas spread far enough they will coalesce into actions that will exponentially grow into larger and larger regenerative change. Learn about all this and so much more in **The Permaculture Student 2: A Collection of Regenerative Solutions**.

We know it's possible. We know how to accomplish it. The only thing standing in our way is ourselves and our habits. It's time to change them and reverse the collapse of our entire life support system, the earth and its ecosystems as we know it.

The time is now.
Go & Regenerate.

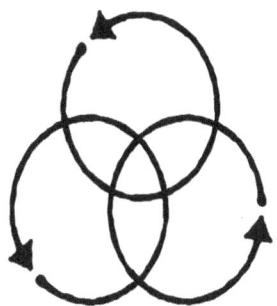

The Advanced Permaculture Student Online
an online course of regenerative solutions & career paths

We've Waited Long Enough
It's Time To Heal Our World & Ourselves!

Join Matt Powers & 70+ Experts in the Regenerative Spectrum of Permaculture
Learn How to Make Permaculture Your Lifestyle & Your Living

Permaculture Design - Holistic Management - Keyline Design - Advanced Soil Science - Large-Scale Land & Ocean Restoration - Social Permaculture - Mycology - Alternative Energy - Aquaculture - Permatecture - Gardening - Food Forestry - Ecological Landscaping - Plant Breeding - HM Grazing - ReGreening Deserts - Urban Permaculture - KNF - Bokashi/EM - Beekeeping - Conservation Hunting - Mead Making - Regenerative Business - Nonviolence - Life Planning - Probiotics - Earthworms & More!

Visit the
ThePermacultureStudent.com

The Permaculture Student 2

a collection of regenerative solutions

The 2nd Edition

> "A landmark in the evolution of human-ecological relationships...
> I highly recommend it."
> — Peter McCoy, Radical Mycology

> "Well researched, articulate and engaging, the Permaculture Student Two
> fills a key niche in the world of permaculture education."
> —Erik Ohlsen, StoryScapes & Permaculture Skills Center

Download The Permaculture Student 2
for FREE at
ThePermacultureStudent.com

About the Author

Matt Powers is an educator, author, seed saver, plant breeder, blogger, podcast host, permaculturist, and family guy helping families, students, and individuals all over the world live more regeneratively, so they can partner with nature in their daily lives. You can find his online courses, curriculum, books, free resources, blog posts, and more at ThePermacultureStudent.com. Catch Matt on iTunes with A Regenerative Future with Matt Powers - new episodes every Monday.

About this Book

This book represents the author's research, own insights, and the insights of many who have come before. To research more in-depth into the concepts and specific examples described in this book (as well as their sources), please reference **The Permaculture Student 2** by Matt Powers which is the product of a collaborative effort involving regenerative experts from across the globe - you can purchase it on ThePermacultureStudent.com and soon on Amazon. This book in many ways is a distillation of all the research that was required to write **The Permaculture Student 2**.

Acknowledgments

Thank you to all that support me, my family, and my work. Together we can make lasting change for a brighter future.

-Matt Powers